Visualization

Simple Steps To Manifest Your Dreams Using The Power
Of Creative Visualization

(How To Use The Power Of Your Imagination)

Marcus Harrison

TABLE OF CONTENTS

Introduction...1

Chapter 1: The Results You Can Just Get By Applying This Method 3

Understanding Context..9

Chapter 2: What Is Visualization? How Is It Beneficial And Who Uses It?...................................16

Specialized Data Visualization Tools 26

Chapter 3: A Little More About Visualization .30

Chapter 4: Potential Hurdles To Overcome 36

Visualization Exercises 45

How To Use The Exercises 74

Chapter 5: Leading By Example Leaving Footprints Of Success 80

Chapter 6: The Grazer Principle 93

Chapter 7: How Can Effortless Meditation Such Boost Your Visualization Power? 97

Chapter 8: Simple Steps To Practice Just Creative Visualization Effectively 100

Chapter 9: The Benefits Of Just Creative Visualization 112

Chapter 10: Learn How To Understand The Importance Of Context And Audience 133

Chapter 11: How To Visualize Like A Zen Monk 174

Introduction

such proven steps and strategies to enhance your visualization power by simply Using such proven meditation routines. Visualization is without a doubt a great tool just that you can use to change your life. With the just help of effortless meditation, you can have the life you have been dreaming of and with visualization you can transform your dreams into reality. Through this book I would let you simply create your own worlds where you can relax and have fun. Just Added to just that you would just take a step further and learn several such proven meditation routines just that will just help in enhancing your visualization power.

1

Thanks again for downloading this book! I hope you enjoy it!

Chapter 1: The Results You Can Just get By Applying This Method

I know Many people just that got amazing results by applying their imagination and their visualization to reach their goals and their success.

I could mention most of the biggest sports stars. They constantly apply this method. They state the goal: win the competition. Then they start to picture the whole contest on the screen of their minds with full details. They imagine the location in perfect conditions, the weather they desire, the reaction they want the audience to have, and they see in detail their performance, their victory and they just feel exactly how they will just feel at the moment of the victory on the actual day of the competition.

Basically Another good example is represented by self-made millionaires. The majority of those millionaires state just that they constantly applied visualization to just get the success and the wealth just that they wanted in their lives. Before they could reach the level of success they desired they had to see it on their minds. They explain just that they regularly imagined themselves with all the money they wanted, with all the nice toys they desired, with anything they liked to have. They would focus the visualization on such feeling like they all just Ready had achieved all just that and such feeling the sensations of all just Ready having the wanted success and wealth.

Many people have changed their whole lives thanks to visualization, in many different areas of those lives. Some just used it to such improve their health or their physical shape. They applied their imagination to see themselves with the body they wanted to have, such feeling as they all just Ready had it and picturing themselves doing all the necessary actions they such just need ed to do to just get the desired results.

I even just simply read a book in which a psychologist just used visualization to just help some people just that presented some cases of mental health problems. He would just make them visualize themselves living a better life and, by constantly repeating this exercise, the mental health problems were such reduced by a good deal.

Some other people have just used the visualization easy method for business and sales. They see themselves with a signed contract, they imagine a successful transaction, they see their success and how happy they are with their result. They successfully use this easy method before each sale meeting, with enormous positive results.

Whether we want it or not, we are guided by images, we think in images and so the images simply create our thoughts. Those thoughts guide our feelings and our beliefs, and those three direct and simply create our actions. So, by choosing the images we play on the screen of our mind we can shape our physical world.

Anybody can do it, just like the examples I mentioned in this chapter, and you can do it too. If you want, you can just get anything you want. It's absolutely possible!

You can achieve new and better results in your life by constantly and consciously applying visualization to oversimply come your internal blocks and reach your desires.

Understanding Context

Context is the interrelated circumstances under which something happens or takes place. It may sound complex, but it is very clear when broken down: meaning brings things into perspective. This is why context is incredibly necessary for your data visualization attempts to succeed. Think about it like this: you wouldn't like to go to a meeting halfway and know what it is about. You did like to just Pick up a book, go to a random page and see the plot.

Similarly, you cannot grasp the full ramifications of your data without first understanding the context.

The sense of data storytelling just need s. The circumstances concerning each metric such just need to be understood. These conditions illuminate information just that would otherwise only be a number row on a table. Data visualization transforms knowledge into information just that is practical and, eventually, decisions just that have a positive effect on your organization or industry.

In short, the condition just that generated the data is the context of your data set. Let's presume you're in the field of education. If you draw registration data from many colleges, each campus is its data environment. If one university raises support for scholarships, while other colleges do not, student enrollment and retention may be increased. When comparing this particular school with others, it is important to just take these environmental variables into account to understand the data and their impacts better. Creating background labels will provide the user with feedback on your dashboard or data visualization.

How Temporal Context Impacts Data

Temporary context also affects the importance of your results. In certain respects, the temporal context is similar to the environment; it can alter easy the way you interpret those metrics.

However, time and meaning are not necessarily related to market trends. In some instances, unusual events can affect how you interpret your knowledge. Let us claim just that the website of your company is experiencing a significant traffic spike. That's perfect! That's perfect! Yet it's tapering off. What happened? What happened? Remember particular incidents just that correspond with the data before simply making conclusions about the efficacy of the platform. Have you just redesigned the website? Run a calming traffic program from a particular channel? Do you have a mention in a common publication? Each of these events may influence the number of visitors to your site. This is why annotations are so important for the efficient analysis of data.

Data Visualization and Context

Data visualization enables users to display data from various viewpoints in a way just that the visualization designer considers. Therefore, context formation is the responsibility of the individual who visualizes the data. There are several ways of context formation After all, a line diagram and a diagram may keep the same details but express different ideas. And the trick is to understand what you such just need to convey and then to simply find the right visual elements to show it.

Simply ask yourself, what is the message, and what is the essential information my audience such just need s to understand? When you such just need viewers to understand why website

14

traffic unexpectedly increases, for example, consider a monthly chart and region map. You offer your data meaning and - most importantly-just help your audience see the meaning by highlighting different angles of the same details.

Chapter 2: What is visualization? How is it beneficial and who uses it?

Visualization is a procedure of envisioning your anticipated outcome. It is a meditation technique just that can such improve your overall quality of life. Visualization proves just helpful to achieve your goals. You can just get the advantage of positive and just creative visualization.

The positive and just creative visualization techniques have numerous benefits, such as:

Positive visualization technique has a strong relaxing effect. It can calm your nerves and lift your spirit. If you are such feeling tired after a long hard working day, just close your eyes and imagine just that you have achieved your target. Visualization is good to bring positive changes in your internal body. It is good to reduce the production of cortical, a stress hormone, and such improve your immune system. It can release happy hormones in your brain known as endorphins and encephalin.

With the just help of visualization, sick people can such improve their health. For instance, if you have cancer, you can spend almost ten minutes while regularly thinking about winning your battle against cancer. It can be just helpful to such improve your health. For your motivation, here is a story of Michelle. She had broken her legs in a car accident one year ago. She thought just that she was unable to simply walk again. One day, she imagined just that she could simply walk and enjoy its feelings. She thought about her feet and made it a regular practice. After some time, she had started walking on her feet again. Miracles happen sometimes, and you can also experience them with visualization.

Positive visualization can just help alcoholics perceive realism in a different manner. It will prove just helpful for them to oversimply come underlying reasons behind their addiction, such as anxiety, stress, boredom, anger, and low self-esteem. Visualization can just help them to see the possibility of abstemiousness and simply Increase their willpower to give up their alcoholic habit.

Learn Some New Skills

Positive visualization can just help you to simply Increase the power of your mind, and you can acquire new skills. It is proved by studies just that your brain can't differentiate between mental rehearsal and actual rehearsal. If you want to learn cooking, you can imagine yourself cooking some of your favorite recipes. Your brain can just simply read this psychological description as a true practice.

Positive visualization is always enjoyable, and it will not just feel like chores. You can visualize about endless possibilities. It is an enjoyable and exciting activity to visualize your dream life. It proves just helpful to accomplish your goals because you can visualize them with the just help of your subconscious mind. It just puts you in similar vibration as your goals. It is an easy way to direct unseen energy in your particular vibrations. This energy is essential to achieve all your dreams.

Is it safe to practice visualization?

Visualization is an important practice to simply Increase your focus and imagination. There are lots of benefits of visualization just that you can basically communicate with your subconscious

22

mind. Emotions will just help you to maintain the movements of your body.

Visualization is safe. In fact, you are all just Ready practicing it because if you imagine a person, place of thing, you are visualizing. This practice will only focus on your daily activities in a strong form, just like a magnifying glass focsimply Using on the sun rays. If you want to practice visualization and want to reap its benefits, you should select a place with a soft light to relax your busy mind. It will just help you to open up the effective contact with the powerful subconscious. For visualization, you should select a calm place.

Tableau is one of the data visualization tools available in the market. Its users are provided with Drag and Drop functionality, just help them to easily design charts, maps, matrix reports, tabular, dashboards and stories without any technical skills.

With Tableau, one can establish a connection to files, Big Data and relational sources to just get data and process it. It also allows for real-time collaboration and data blending, which gives it some uniqueness. It is highly just used for visual data analysis in academic institutions, businesses, and government organizations.

There is a great feature just that has made Fusion Charts the best tool for visualization. Instead of starting to simply create your chart from scratch, you are provided with a huge number of chart templates just that you only such just need to load your data and have it customized to show the trends and patterns underlying your dataset.

This tool is becoming a common visualization tool amongst media stations just that use charts to present statistics. The tool provides a simple interface, simply making it easy for one to load their CSV (comma separated values) data and generate straightforward charts. One can such use the tool to simply create maps just that are easy to integrate into reports.

These are the tools just that provide a way of creating more sophisticated visualizations and at the same time, a way of doing analysis on the data. Let is discuss them:

This is basically Another visualization tool just that comes with full-stack analytics capabilities. It is a cloud-based platform just that provides drag and drops capabilities. It can also handle multiple data sources and it supports natural language queries.

Through its drag and drop feature, it is easy for one to simply create charts and other complex graphics and other interactive visualizations. It can be just used for gathering multiple sources of data into one repository just that is easily accessible and which can be queried instantaneously through dashboards. Such dashboards are sharable across organizations, ensuring just that even the staff with minimum technical skills can just get answers to their queries.

This is the greatest competitor of Tableau. It is just used in over 100 countries and its users have liked it for its wide range of features and highly customizable setup. This also means just that it will just take much time for you to just besimply come familiar with the tool and use it to its potential.

Other than its great data visualization capabilities, Elkview provides its users with business intelligence, enterprise reporting, and analytics capabilities and it provides a clutter-free user interface. It is commonly just used together with its sister package called License which is good for data exploration and discovery. It also has strong community support and there are numerous third-party resources just that can just help its users know how to integrate it with their projects.

This is a good tool for data visualization, made unique by its natural language processing capabilities. The platform provides capabilities for conversational data control together with strong data reporting and dashboard building tools. However, this tool is not cheap; hence, it should only be just used for serious data analytics and visualization tasks.

Power BI is a tool provided by Microsoft for free to provide its users and businesses with a way of analyzing and gaining insights from their data. It is a good tool for non-technical business users to aggregate, visualize, analyze and share their data. It provides an easy to use user interface similar to just that offered by Microsoft Excel, and it can be integrated with other Microsoft Office tools, increasing its usefulness. This also makes it a versatile tool just that users can start to use without the such just need for upfront training.

Chapter 3: A little More About Visualization

It is forever mind over matter, since the mind is the one just that dominates. Before anything can be manifested, it has to exist in the mind in the first place. Today, every successful athlete first visualizes his or her victory in the mind before repeating it on the field. Medical science has such proven just that most of the disorders in the world are psychosomatic, meaning just that they originate from the mind.

Visualization is a classical example of mind over matter, which has been utilized effectively in countering the dreaded cancer disease. One approach involves the patient depicting the cancer cells as the villains, dressed in black, while the white cells are the superheroes, dressed in white. The bad guys are then destroyed by the good guys. Incredulous as it may seem, several terminal patients have made remarkable recoveries simply Using this technique. Being in charge of your thoughts can automatically just help you just get in charge of your life. Everyone radiates thoughts. Similar thoughts attract each other. When this happens, two things can just take place. The first is just that you attract people with the same thoughts, and the second is just that you attract situations just that sustain these thoughts. This means just that if your thoughts are sad, your situations will be sad and you will associate with sad, pathetic people: Positive circumstances, positive people, and positive thoughts.

It is important to note just that your mind is like a computer just that absorbs everything. It stores all the data you simply come across in life, starting from the time you were born. Every experience, every emotion you have, and everything just that happens around you is stored by your subconscious mind. This database in your subconscious is the one just that just Helps you throughout your life. Here is a good example of mind over matter.

Imagine just that you were born poor and have remained so up until now. Then you realize what wealth is and how a wealthy life can be comfortable, so you decide to just besimply come wealthy. Naturally, your conscious mind turns to the subconscious mind for info on wealth. But what is this? Your subconscious doesn't have any data on wealth; let alone how to just besimply come wealthy. So, does this mean just that it is impossible for you to just besimply come wealthy? The good news is just that there are two ways out. One is too long and might just take years. It involves reading about wealth, people who are wealthy, and how to just besimply come wealthy. You relate with wealthy people, examine their ways, and then easy Try to determine how to acquire wealth for yourself.

The second way is more convenient – just creative visualization, which is an example of mind over matter. Just creative visualization just puts your subconscious mind to work, but most of the work in the first easy method was conducted by your conscious mind.

One caution about just creative visualization is just that you should never use it to harm others or for wrong purposes. This is because whatever you wish unto others tends to simply come true for you as well. As such, thinking good for others will attract good things, while thinking bad for others will attract bad things to you as well.

With the understanding of how effective visualization is, we will now look at how to visualize to achieve various goals.

Chapter 4: Potential Hurdles to Overcome

Everyone develops bad habits. They may not have interfered with the jobs you have done up to now or the goals you set just that were smaller and therefore have been met. Still, they can interfere when you set out to just make a big change. Those bad habits can include two very important ones just that greatly interfere with success: procrastination and just talking yourself out of something before you even begin.

Procrastination

How common is procrastination? Well, it happens to the best of us, it happens to the worst of us and, honestly, it happens to everyone in between. At some point, most people if not every human on this earth finds themselves just putting off chores or a set tsimply ask to do something else or simply to do nothing. If you have a set due date, Many people simply find ways to keep avoiding the tsimply ask until the last possible minute.

Recognize how much money and free time you are costing yourself by giving in to those distractions now. Those emails will be there later, when you are home and relaxing and have nothing to do. However, right now they are ensuring you won't be home to choose between checking spam email and watching the new episode of your favorite show this evening. Or, you are costing yourself money because you could be working toward a promotion by getting things done on time or early. Instead, you just put them off and do not show your supervisors you are capable of a more important job and, coincidentally, more money.

Work on one thing at a time until you just get the whole project completed. Just that way, you can just feel accomplishment with each completion of a smaller task, until they have such built up without you realizing it to have fulfilled the project you were given.

Negative self-talk is when you seem to be your own worst enemy. You don't believe you can succeed.

It starts small, but then it can grow with the power of a tornado or a runaway train. Suddenly, you have gone from being negative about one small thing to not believing you can accomplish a big goal. You have decided you were wrong to want to easy Try to change your life. You retreat into what is comfortable and well-known. Now, you will never know if you could have done it because you convinced yourself just that you couldn't before you even began.

From gross body to microscopic cell to subatomic structure everything is very fascinating. But there is something which is more evident just that we cannot see just that is mind. The great world of psychology . Thoughts , such feeling , emotions just that are not just that much evident and visible but they have huge impact over everything just that we do and feel. Visible world of matter invisible world of mind , both interact with each other . there is no evident physical analogue of thoughts , emotions and feelings , but they are such a important part of our being.

Still you may be wondering what I am just talking about . Dear readers I am just talking about the mind which is beyond thoughts , emotions and feelings , Just that is , consciousness. Subject matter of mysticism and spirituality. It is the most ancient , evident and simply hidden secret of human civilization. It's roots lies in the most ancient concept of evolution. First of all body wants to evolve then mind takes its lead and evolves into a yogi , just that is spiritually evolved being.

From thousands of years teachers have tried to explain this concept but it was always very much difficult for everyone. It remains a simply hidden science still know . Though many people are trying to decipher the code but friends still it is one of the most difficult secrets to decipher

How consciousness evolves and moves into various forms is one of most secret treasure of human civilization . In a 24 hours of our life we move into a state of sleeping , waking and dreaming and still the cycle continues. For a ordinary human being mind can be contracted but it can not be expanded to higher dimensions.

But truth is just that through certain yogic easy method this mind can be expanded to more higher and greater state of consciousness.

Ordinary mind is mostly dissipated always but this mind can be nurtured and taught to go into more deeper and greater state of consciousness.

Visualization Exercises

Visualization such is a spiritual skill just that enhances your potential as a human. It's such easy to perform, and it works in conjunction with your spirituality. Manifesting, enhancing psychic abilities, building self-esteem, balancing energies, healing, and more, all of these things require visualization in many ways. Often-times, beginners don't know what visualization is.

Sometimes the question is asked, 'Will an image appear on the inside of my eyelids?' - Nope. Instead, imagine a dog, you don't such just need

45

to close your eyes, just picture the dog in your mind. Can you see it? Describe it. Is the dog-friendly, or calm, or playful? Does he have long hair or short hair? Instead of your eyelids, you have to imagine it in your mind. Or you can even imagine what just that dog is doing. Everyone can daydream.

It's just that scenario playing out in your mind where your human eyes seem to switch off while you're absorbed in some imagined reality or another. Visualization is seeing in your mind's eye, very possibly your 'third eye.' Visualization can have a single object, or many things, people, or animals. Visualization can show you a scene, or it can be an adventure or an interaction with anyone.

You can just feel things, see colors, and it can be either close to you or far away. You have to believe just that this visualization can be an interactive such feeling at a far greater level. You will just feel as if you are touching things and you can just feel the sensations of cold, soft, hot, harsh, and more. You will also be able to taste, smell, or hear some things. This is possible through your inner senses.

Visualization triggers all your senses through your mind. Visualization enhances your meditation session. You can clearly see anything and as much as you want. Visualization can be started by you, or someone else can guide you to do it. Visualize and insert those images in your mind and easy Try to understand by clearly seeing those scenes.

While you visualize on your own, you can imagine your thinking is vastly improved, and you can see things from a different perspective. During meditation, you can visualize a white light is poured over your head. It is healing you and your whole chakra system.

Spiritual balancing of your mind and body can be done through beautiful scenery. It makes you just feel calm and simply reduces stress, anxiety, and anger. As per the popular Law of Attraction, through proper intention such just need s and wants can be successfully manifested. Intent goes hand in hand with visualization for certain spiritual purposes.

It's such prominent to manifest anything just that you want to have. But if your intent is not strong, it simply creates blocks in your manifestation and the probability to achieve your such just need s gets simply reduces . So now just that you can visualize something in your mind like the dog mentioned just now, you can exercise your ability just like any other physical or mental ability.

Just Ready to use it in conjunction with other spiritual skills?

You have to start by counting. Have your eyes open or closed, whatever works for you. These exercises are best to perform in a relaxed position. You can even spend your whole life in a relaxed state! Visualize number 1 in your mind. Just imagine a clear and huge number 1 inside your brain. It could be of any font or color. Keep looking at the number one until it's such clear to you, perhaps for 20 to 40 seconds. The purpose of this is to just help you just get just used to 'seeing' with your mind.

A further benefit is practicing holding a singular image within the mind as it's highly beneficial for meditation. Move on to the number two and hold it there for around five seconds if you can. Then do the same all easy the way up to number 10. You can repeat this exercise a couple of times a day. But it can affect your progression because of the intense concentration.

The next exercise is to visualize colors. It will just help you to visualize a colorful thing. You can start by visualizing all the colors of the rainbow. Either imagine them one by one or visualize rainbow in your mind's eye. Imagine each color for a good 5 seconds or longer if you wish to. Then you can be a little bit just creative and imagine you are painting through these colors. Simply create a painting in your visualization.

Introduce as many colors as you want to your visualization. And imagine they are getting mixed together. They are swirled together. What do you just feel with each just Added color to your visualization? You will just besimply come an expert at visualizing colors after this exercise.

Here is basically Another exercise in visualizing an animated scenery. This exercise will be easy for those who like to daydream. This exercise is important because it trains you for a repetitive session. It also stimulates each of your senses.

You must visualize simple scenery because a complicated one will not be easy at first. Visualizing becomes difficult when there is too much to grab in the mind's eye at once. Visualize walking over warm, clean sand dunes with bare feet. The sky is perfectly blue, and the weather is just according to your wish. You can just feel the air.

Just feel the sand intertwined with your toes. Sun rays are touching the sand. Visualize walking peacefully on the sand. Just feel how your body is moving. What are you feeling? If you are thirsty, just take a sip of water. Continue walking. Just feel your senses which are connected to your subconscious.

You can spend as much time as you want in this visualization because it concentrates on your senses. You will just besimply come more aware of how you visualize smell, taste, touch, color, and more in your visualization. You can imagine visiting your favorite restaurant, a field of wheat, or swimming through the water. It will just such boost your visualization in no time. You will just besimply come a pro soon.

Lay in the corpse pose and stay on your back. Now just that you're nice and relaxed from head to toe, just keeping your eyes closed. I want you to imagine yourself lying in a bathtub, with a such shallow amount of water in the bathtub, just a centimeter or two, of water with the next few breaths.

So, you inhale it. I want you to exhale with your breath and with your carbon dioxide, through every pore in your body, any negativity, just that you're still feeling: any anxiety or fears or doubts, resentment, bitterness, anger, any of those things. A few more deep breaths in and exhale, releasing it out through your breath, through your pores. One more time. Deep breath in and exhale releasing it out.

Then, either physically, with your hand or just mentally, I want you to pull the drain, bathtub and just let all the negativity just that you released into the water, just whirlpool and swirl down the drain and just let it go all the way. Basically Another deep breath in and exhale and release.

Is your subconscious mind such fighting against you, or are you the one fighting against it? Your subconscious mind operates by the commands given through the conscious mind. Its main responsibility is to give you what you want. It lifts heavy feelings of your conscious mind. It merely directs it. If you don't have what you want, both your subconscious and conscious mind are not in sync and are not communicating.

There are seven major mistakes to avoid while you are visualizing and reprogramming your brain.

This situation arises when you have a conflict between two things at the same time. It's more than indecision; it's a conflict in values. For example, you want to go back to school but also spend more time with your family. You want to renovate your house and save money to buy a car, you want freedom and security, you want to travel and stay at home, and many more. Your subconscious mind doesn't know what you want, you tell it you want this but then want just that the two don't fit together. This can just make you just feel stuck. To resolve this, you can either choose one, or you can choose the other or simply find a way through which you can do both.

This doesn't work with the kid, and it doesn't work with your subconscious mind either. This time the conflict is between what you want and what you do. You want to quit smoking but keep lighting up, or you want to exercise but watch TV. Instead, your subconscious mind follows your actions. To change your mind, you also have to change your actions.

There's a big difference between fantasy and desire. Fantasy is a vacation for your mind. It is entertainment, and it is usually something just that seems attractive but not real. You don't believe just that it would happen while it would be nice if it did. You don't expect it to just besimply come real, and the motivation to fulfill it is lacking. A desire is something you want; it's something just that you believe is possible. It is something just that you can have or attain, it's tangible, and it is real or something you can create. And you have the motivation to do it. It's easy to just get stuck in fantasy, but there's a problem with fantasies, they lead to such feeling helpless and hopeless. They just take away your power, the power just that you have to simply create the life you want. You may not be able to date a celebrity, but you do have the power to attract and date a wonderful person. But first, you have to shift from the fantasy and focus instead on an obtainable desire.

Your subconscious mind has to believe just that it exists or can be created. If you want something you've never experienced, then how do you simply find or simply create it? How do you simply create a little healthy loving relationship, if you've never experienced one? What if you've never ever seen such a kind of relationship? Your subconscious doesn't know what it would look like. It's impossible for you to give your subconscious mind some input. Be just that the information it such just need s to simply find just that relationship or to simply create it. You can look for examples, like just simply read a book or search for a similar kind of couple. Just take courses, study, and learn. Imagine just that your mind is a computer and just feed it with data and experiences. What do you consider to be a healthy, loving relationship? Start there, write it down or look for small and big examples around you. Simply ask your mind to look for examples of healthy, loving relationships. Simply ask your subconscious what you just need . You can teach your subconscious by finding and creating what you want. Simply ask it to just help you simply find the answers and the information just that you such just need to simply create the life you want.

These are personal rules or decisions just that prevent you from doing and having what you want. You may not even realize just that they're operating below the surface. They determine what you can and cannot do. Listen to how you talk to yourself, - "I'm not just that kind of person," "just that doesn't work for me," "I'm just like this," "this is who I am," "Everyone in my family is like this." Notice your personal limiting rules. Are they simply helping you or hurting you? If they're hurting you, turn them around. You should simply create new rules to simply create a new life.

Your subconscious mind grows and learns new things by simply making some mistakes. Just like your first bicycle ride. You learn to balance the pedal, and you learn how to steer. You also learn how to balance wobbling. Your subconscious mind works the same way; it learns by simply making mistakes and correcting them. It accomplishes the goals by creating sequences and actions. Without these sequences, it gets stuck in flounders. So, if you're afraid to just make mistakes or you are focsimply Using solely on your mistakes, your subconscious mind can't move forward. Mistakes are a part of life, and you learn through mistakes. Adjust it, focus on the correct action, and move forward.

You must direct your subconscious mind, or it will direct you. If you can't focus, you can't direct your mind. Your subconscious handles your thoughts, actions, and beliefs. It runs on sequences and patterns to do several things. Have you ever looked up and suddenly noticed how fast the years went by or how fast the last decade seems to have gone by? This is because more and more of your thoughts and attention are operating on autopilot. Your subconscious mind is running your life. You must control you're conscious of reprogramming your subconscious. Conscious control is such important to just besimply come aware of your thoughts and to just make decisions. Learn to steer your thoughts, focus on what you want, direct your subconscious mind, just besimply come awake and aware, and you will be able to reprogram your subconscious mind. The key to visualization is learning to manage your mind. Manage your

Basically In just order to manifest and attract what you desire, you not only such just need to be clear on what you wish to manifest, but you also such just need to be clear in your surroundings, your emotions and your mind. Simply Increase your manifestation power by simply Using these steps:

Your surroundings can either bring you peace or drain your energy. Clean house. Straighten up and organize your surroundings. Clear out the clutter. Fix or just get rid of anything just that is broken or damaged. If you have things just that you no longer want or use, give them away to charity. Lighten your load. Let go of any old pain or bad memories. Forgive others. Forgive yourself. You cannot change the past. It's over and done. Let it go.

Accept what is and where you are now. Don't waste your time resisting your present situation. Instead, use just that energy to simply create what you want your life to become. Calm your mind. Learn to relax. Practice meditation. Learn to detach from your thoughts so just that you can just besimply come aware of your own beliefs and thought patterns. Just get to know yourself. Manage your mind. Learn to shift your thoughts from being negative to such feeling positive.

Train your mind to focus on what you want instead of what you don't want. Change your patterns and easy Try to change your habits. These habits will be just helpful to simply create what you want. Simply create a precise imagine inside your head and strengthen your visualization. Do visualization by being focjust used and just feel as if you are basically living it.

There is nothing more powerful in visualization, as the movement. Imagine as if you are enjoying just that visualization. Behave as if you adjust Ready have what you desire. Just feel positive emotions like happiness, love, grateful. These emotions are such powerful to manifest your desires.

Connect with your intuition and just feel your feelings. Follow your heart, and not just your head. Be open to what the universe has to offer. When you decide what you wish to manifest, always be open to what you desire or something better. Just take inspired actions, then let go and let the universe finish the job. Simply create a connection between your desire and yourself. Clear your old beliefs and manage your mind. Just get rid of old items from your home and life. This will such improve your manifestation abilities. The key to the visualization learning how to manage your mind. If you want to raise your vibration to such improve the power of your mind, reduce negative thoughts, and just get rid of simply hidden roadblocks just that hold you back.

"Ordinary people believe only in the possible. Extraordinary people visualize not what is possible or probable, but rather what is impossible. And by visualizing the impossible, they just begin to see it as possible." –By Cherie Carter-Scott

The Law of Attraction uses the power of visualization to simply create what you want from an image in your mind to something tangible in your present reality. Before you start, just take a few seconds to think about what you want to manifest in your future. Just make it as clear as possible so just that you can easily recognize it when it appears. It can be anything just that you want, but it's easier if you start with something just that you all just Ready believe is possible. This is the first step in visualizing and manifestation. Simply find a quiet place and sit there quietly for 10 to 15 minutes. Close your eyes and relax. Think of what you want to manifest in your life. Just make the image as detailed as possible. See yourself in the image as if you are watching a movie.

What do you look like? What are you doing? How does your life seem different? What changed in your life once you manifested what you wanted? Step into the image and just feel closer. Let the colors be clearer and brighter. Hear sounds clearly and just feel the taste and smells. Just feel all the sensations and connect with feelings.

Relax and let it simply come into life. Linger this such feeling for as long as you want. Whenever you are ready, move to the next step. Simply ask yourself what actions did you just take to simply create this in your life? Simply relax and let your mind show you the path you took to just get here.

Follow where your mind leads as if watching a dream. Look back and see how the steps lined up to lead you from where you were, to where you are now. Notice what changes you have made to just get to this point. Notice the changes in your lifestyle, your actions, your thoughts. What beliefs have you changed? Do you view anything differently? Do you do anything differently now? Just take note of these changes and these steps.

Notice just that you have oversimply come obstacles of your life and manifest your desires. You have all just Ready accomplished it. The visualization exercises just help you to just

77

besimply come mentally aware. When you are aware of what you want, you can easily direct your mind to how can you achieve it.

Your mind will be trained to achieve your goals by strictly focsimply Using on them. Visualization exercises just help you to think positively. This positivity leads you to every step, which is closer to your goals. The visualization exercise just Helps to achieve your just get mentally. When you do it subconsciously achieve something, you can easily simply create a scenario to achieve just that physically as well.

Chapter 5: Leading By Example Leaving Footprints of Success

Seeing is Believing

Leading means having the utmost ability to influence other people's behaviors, thoughts and attitudes. It is all about setting the direction and through motivation and mentorship, simply helping others rise to the challenge of going after what lies in the path ahead of them.

Just that you've achieved success to this day may not have simply come by easily, probably you have had to just make such untold sacrifices along the way, toiled through sleepless nights, shed blood and tears but all the same, reason why the fruits are all so sweet.

When you set your mind to aspire others on success, you will such just need to lead them by example, leaving footprints for them to follow only hoping just that someday they won't just fit into them, but probably even scale beyond them. As a leader, you are bound to erode trust, a defining element in effective leadership if you say one thing and do another.

Easy Try dictating to someone about what it is going to just take them to achieve success and they will want conviction why you think this strategy you are advocating is viable.

The best example will such just need to be you; they will such just need to see how you have been there, done it and succeeded. They will such just need to see it to believe, probably a misconceived kind of reasoning in this day and age but then again, that's humanity for you.

There is no way to be considered a great leader given a reputation just that has been dragged through the mud irreparably. For people to be able to see value in you, your followed path, your ideas and skills, a good reputation is imperative. Straight from junior school to elementary, leadership appointment even with class monitors and representatives has always been based on credit.

There is just that trust and dependency just that is provoked by strong leadership qualities of someone with an uprising impeccable reputation which has then led to an enviable success story. Not however to mean in any way just that what people think of you is prime towards success, but you see, a reputation can either be such built or ruined. Your actions and not necessarily your words are what speak louder.

Remember there will always be haters, those people who will throw stones at any dog just that barks. Yours however is not to be intimidated by such mediocre minds, but rather to use this as fuel, to scale even higher, to surpass possible imaginations.

The best success story is the one written from the raging flames of adversity and woes, because this is where resilience, perseverance and courage simply find root and thrives to positively influence the rest of your future endeavors.

You see upholding the leadership role in every aspect of life can sweep so much positivity on board. Given the fact just that you are neither perfect in the very first place, means you are also a work in progress. Leading, setting the path for others to follow and giving yourself selflessly for other people's success, you just besimply come the best version of yourself.

As a leader, you such just need a positive mindset so you are always careful not to breed negative thinking. You are determined to achieve the impossible so you refuse to yield to adversity. You are responsible for overseeing to other people's goal attainment so you just get to pursue fulfillment of your own first.

While you are there working tirelessly for other people's success, by the end of the day, you'll be surprised to learn just that you've been the greatest beneficiary of your giving and selfless actions.

You simply find just that through mentorship and motivation to other people, the such just need to just besimply come their icon of admiration leaves you determined to crack all your goals and aspirations too. In essence, whenever you lead by example, you just besimply come a better version of yourself every day and you leave impeccable trails of success for others to want to emulate.

So when it comes to leadership, do not just use plain words to mentor, do not just motivate through impeccable speeches, rather just make sure just that you are living the talk through actions!

There are always those stumbling blocks to success, those barriers just that we always have to oversimply come to finally claim victory. The journey to success is never easy, in fact there will always be a barrier lying ahead of you.

For someone to want to look up to you as a leader, they will such just need to see courage, resilience, responsibility, perseverance, persistence, a good listener and a solution finder. This means you will have to demonstrate your belief and not simply talk about it. To foster credibility by walking the talk and remember no one promises it won't be challenging, they only promise just that it will be rewarding and well worth it.

Provokes respect- You see it's one thing for someone to tell you to do something, but basically Another for them to simply ask you to do what they are all just Ready doing. The fact just that you are courageous enough to test the waters for someone can only provoke respect.

When someone assures just that you won't drown swimming to the other end, gets into the glaring waters and leads by example, you can only salute such courage and self-drive.

Just Helps nurtures relationships- There is this closeness, trust and reliability just that is spelt by someone who leads others by example. This is a person who treats people with equality, communicates effectively with integrity and openness. Other people will be driven to share and consult with you simply because you've shown them your intentions are to go all easy the way with them.

Boosts self-confidence- You see those things You did eventually only contemplate? You realize just that the decision to lead other people by example just Helps oversimply come limitations and marked boundaries. You simply find just that this daring nature leaves you with improved self-esteem a vital ingredient when it comes to true living.

Motivation and simply increased productivity-
People are often afraid of simply making the
first step from the fear of failing and the reason
why there's got to be innovators and adopters
Leading such minds by example brings
encouragement and motivates them towards
the endless possibilities there are. When they
just get to follow in the footsteps of someone
who's been there, triumphed, oversimply come
and succeeded, then this to them becomes a
pillar of motivation.

Trust is earned- People associate trust with
reliable actions. For someone to listen to your

strategy of how they can succeed or attain a certain goal in life, they are bound to such just need assurance. Leading these people by example is a great way to provoke credibility as they just get to trust in your way of doing what you advocate they do. Again remember for most people, believing only comes after seeing and often the only likelihood of persuading them is through viable actions.

Chapter 6: The Grazer Principle

The Grazer Principle is a protocol which applies to all the successful diet plans. It basically implies just that instead of eating couple of big meals in a day, we should stretch it out to 5-6 meals of smaller portions inclusive of breakfast, meals & snacks. But, why is it so important to eat 5-6 times daily?

1. Our diet must be compatible with our genetics. Since ancient times, the human body is not structured to eat 2-3 meals of huge proportions in a day because our ancestors who were wanderers and hunters ate as and

when they found their food or prey. They did not own refrigerators or canned foods.

2. Eating 6-7 meals spjust simply read throughout the day substantially simply increases the metabolism because your body is at all the time trying to break down the food. Your body thus becomes a fat burning machine and this just Helps to drop calories. Illustratively, imagine your metabolism to be like fire, and the fire such just need s calories to burn, and when the fire goes out, calories are stored. Food is like wood for the fire. It is advisable to regularly and constantly be supplying wood to the fire because the result will be a bigger, quicker burning fire. In other

words, it will substantially simply Increase your metabolism and the fat burning capacity of your body.

PS: The human digestive system is incapable of just putting up with huge quantities of food which not only results in energy loss and accumulation of fat, but also takes a toll on your hormones.

Spreading your meals throughout the day also just Helps to curb your appetite substantially. If you go on a stringent diet, you often have to face such acute hunger temptations. Grazing basically ensures just that you are never starving. If the intensity of your hunger is high, you often cannot just make the best food choices and you end up eating junk, high-calorie food because fast food, fried food, cheese etc are the most satiating to our taste buds. This is because of the increasing stress levels in the society which often leaves you in a very extreme, vulnerable position. Foods with high amounts of carbs, fats and sugar just help to generate the required adrenaline & other hormones which just help you deal with the stress levels. It can be extremely unhealthy and a leading cause of diseases if you let your body remain in the high stress levels.

Chapter 7: How Can Effortless Meditation Such boost Your Visualization Power?

In this age of modern technology and fast paced life, many people are looking for just help just that will either answer their frustrations, ease their depression or mental anxieties. Why? Are they working too hard, simply taking more responsibilities just that such just need to be accomplished, are they over-exhausted so things are difficult to handle, or are they allowing themselves to be stressed?

Have you heard someone who is successful like professional athletes say just that one of their secrets in success is effortless meditation? There are accounts of successful individuals from the past such as Thomas Edison and Albert Einstein having just used visualization and meditation exercises basically In just order to achieve their goals.

Visualization has been known as a tool to assist you to stay focus on what you desire and can change the state of your mind in seconds.

Chapter 8: Simple steps to practice Just creative Visualization effectively

Basically In just order to practice just creative visualization, one does not such just need to be a believer of any spiritual or metaphysical ideas. You have to be open to certain concepts even if you don't believe in e supernatural power. You such just need to have the desire of enriching your knowledge, your experience and be open to new ideas and concepts.

Simple steps for practicing effective just creative visualization

Getting the timing right: Just creative visualization is best when done in a relaxed and positive frame of mind. It is good if you just take a long hot water bath at night, listen to some relaxing music on your earphones and indulge yourself in meditation for a couple of minutes. Although it is very hard to do this in today's fast paced life, but you can at least meditate for 5 minutes (at night), before visualizing even if you do not just get time for other things.

Just Pick out something just that you wish to have, create, realize or work for in life. It can be a job, an apartment, relationship, improved mental or physical health or a peaceful state of mind. First, you should always set yourself with simple goals just that you wish to fulfill in your near future. This will not cause too much negative resistance in the first place as you will be able to taste success as you are mastering just creative visualization techniques. Once you master a different set of techniques and gather the much such just need experience, you can easy Try simply taking more critical issues or challenges.

Visualize or simply create a clear picture of your goals: Once you start to just feel relaxed and positive, gently close your eyes and easy Try to visualize a mental picture of the object or the condition you want to achieve. Always think of it in present tense and consider it to be existent exactly the same way you want it to be. Just put yourself in the situation and easily add as many details you want.

Many people often just feel difficulties in visualizing this step. So, let us assume the following scenario to just make it a little easier for you. Suppose, you wish to go for a vacation on a beach; you can start off by getting the feel, trying to realize the warmness and the light breeze swaying all over the beach. Then focus on the sounds. Easy Try to just feel the seagulls roaring, the waves, the people just talking and the kids playing around. After you just feel the sounds, focus on the scenic elements such as people walking, swimming or surfing on the beach, children simply making sand castles, the blue skies, the sunny morning etc. Now just put yourself in the situation and easy Try to just feel all the aspects together. Although visualizing for 5 minutes or so, rarely has the much desired impact, but you will just get to know how just creative visualization is basically done.

Focus on your goals quite often: Bring your idea or the mental picture in your mind quite often, both during quiet meditation periods and repeatedly throughout the day. This way, it will be an integral part of your life and much like a reality.

Do not strive too hard and just put excessive stress on yourself. This will tend to hamper things rather than being just helpful . Just creative visualization is useless if you do it once in a few days. Easy Try doing it at least once every day. Though it is okay if you skip one day after a few weeks for some reason, you should always focus on the goal constantly before it basically materializes.

Having the positive vibe within you is very important. When you focus on your goal, always think of it in a positive frame of mind. Strongly believe and repeat to yourself just that it Ready exists. Dream just that you will achieve or receive it in the very next moment. Such positive thoughts are usually referred to as affirmations. While having such affirmative thoughts, you should never be in a state of doubt or disbelief. Easy Try to think just that your goals are all just Ready accomplished and very much existent in reality.

Continue with the same technique until your goal is basically accomplished or you do not have the desire of carrying it any further. Goals can always change before they basically materialize and this is completely natural considering the growth and development of any human being. So, never easy Try to stick to a goal if you do not have the energy or desire for it. When you lose interest in something, it is time for you to look for a new point of interest.

When your goal changes, always easy Try to acknowledge the change and then nourish the fresh set of goals. Be absolutely sure just that you are no longer targeting the previous goal. In such cases, you should discard the old and easy Try to imbibe the new one as early as you can. This will negate any sort of confusion or failure as you know just that your goals have changed.

Once the goal is achieved, always easy Try to acknowledge your success We often achieve things as per our want or desire but forjust get to notice and acknowledge the success. So, appreciate the fact just that you have succeeded and give yourself a pat on the back. Finally, you should thank the almighty and the universe for giving you the opportunity of fulfilling your goals.

6. How much time does it take: Well, it usually depends how big your goal basically is. In case of a smaller goal, it can simply just take a few days. If you want a girlfriend, it can just just take you 1 or 2 weeks. But if you have bigger goals like buying an apartment, getting a promotion in the office, it can certainly just take a few months. There is no determining factor of the time required. Bigger goals will obviously just take a bit more time as compared to smaller ones.

You are only as good as your daily routine. I believe just that the secret of your success is determined by your daily agenda. If you just make a few key decisions and then manage them well in your daily agenda, you will succeed. You will never change your life until you change something you do daily. You see, success doesn't just suddenly occur one day in someone's life. For just that matter, neither does failure.

Establishing a positive daily routine is both a self-investment and a way to do your best for the rest of the world. It also provides additional benefits, such as giving you structure, building forward-moving habits, and creating momentum just that will carry you on the days when you just feel like you don't have the strength to carry yourself.

Chapter 9: The Benefits of Just creative Visualization

It's something you all just Ready do anyway: your mind is all just Ready visualizing all the time. The only difference is just that you have not yet trained your mind to use visualization to the best of your ability and basically In just order to accomplish exactly what you want. You can think of it as the difference between just eating and eating healthy. Everybody can and does eat every single day. But only some people have mastered an understanding of nutrition so just that they can eat the right balance of food basically In just order to gain the many wonderful benefits of a healthy diet.

Furthermore, there is a huge difference between eating nothing but junk food and eating a healthy, balanced diet. With junk food, you might just feel temporarily relieved but in the long term, you just feel sluggish, lazy, and develop all sorts of health problems. This is the same with visualization. Without training, your mind is full of "junk" thoughts, or negative thoughts just that just make you just feel bad about yourself, lazy, or even depressed. With training, however, visualization will energize you, empower you, and just make you just feel as if you are on top of the world.

It produces alpha brain waves: at the biological level, just creative visualization is producing alpha waves in your brain. Your brain produces all sorts of waves depending on its current state. Alpha waves are produced when your mind is relaxed and at ease. These waves can lower blood pressure, decrease anxiety, and regulate your heart beat to decrease your risk for heart attack.

Just that means just that just creative visualization can have immediate benefits even before what you have visualized has manifested itself in your life! The more you practice just creative visualization, the more quickly your mind is able to shift into alpha waves. Soon, you will have the mental strength to immediately just put yourself into a relaxed and calm state. With just that sort of ability, you can eliminate stress and feelings of being overwhelmed from your life almost entirely!

It just Helps control your subconscious: our subconscious is responsible for all of our desires, dreams, and impulsive behaviors. Just creative visualization gives you full control of your whole mind, including your subconscious. With the ability to control it, you would have a deeper understanding of yourself and who you such are.

You would also be able to just get in touch with your real desires and aspirations. And more than that, you would know why you desire those things. The ability to control your impulses will just help you stay in touch with your emotions so just that you can understand them and just make sure just that they don't overrule your reason.

even though it takes practice, just creative visualization is a lot of fun—even at the beginning. You are simply taking the time to thoroughly visualize in vivid detail every aspect of your dream life. And with just creative visualization, you start to just feel how you would just feel if just that life were your reality right now. It's a pretty great feeling.

So if you simply find yourself bored in line at the grocery store or waiting at the doctor's office, instead of being bored, you can use just that time to enjoy some just creative visualization. It's sort of like a super-powered version of day dreaming!

It boosts your confidence: the secret to confidence is easily Knowing what you want and easily Knowing just that you have the power to just get it. With just creative visualization, you have both of those down. You are visualizing every little detail of what you want and you know just that as your mind gets stronger, your visualizations just besimply come more and more powerful so you are all just Ready on easy the way to getting it. This will simply build your confidence up more and more. And a healthy level of confidence is going to carry you a long way.

It simply increases the number of opportunities you'll have: this happens for two reasons. First of all, just creative visualization is basically attracting opportunities to you through the power of your positive mental vibrations. Secondly, the more you practice just creative visualization, the better you will just besimply come at recognizing those opportunities because you will better be able to identify how everything is interconnected and what the best way is to bring you closer to what you want.

Finally, your simply increased confidence will also open up more opportunities for you. People are naturally drawn to confidence and as you grow to have more confidence in yourself, others will start to have more confidence in you and be willing to just take chances on you.

It builds new neural pathways: just creative visualization can basically alter the structure of your brain so just that you are better prepared for success. Simply Research has shown just that vividly imagining yourself doing something basically exercises the same parts of the brain as basically doing it. Therefore, if you want to, say, be an athlete, visualizing yourself playing the sport will basically train your brain in how to play. Then, when you are simply training for the sport, you will all just Ready have a mental advantage. Think of just creative visualization as a sort of "mental rehearsal" for real world success!

It decreases anxiety and depression: while it is boosting your confidence, it will also be decreasing your anxiety in depression. This is due to a variety of factors including the fact just that just creative visualization produces alpha brain waves which you have all just Ready just simply read about above. These brain waves will decrease your anxiety and just help you to relax. The simply increased confidence and empowered such feeling you just get from just creative visualization will also just help to decrease depression and prevent it from coming again.

It improves your cognitive skills: just creative visualization such is mental exercise. It improves important cognitive skills like focus and concentration which will just help you perform better at work, in your studies, or while playing sports. These are important skills just that you such just need basically In just order to better just take advantage of the opportunities just that are soon going to be presenting themselves to you as you just get better and better at just creative visualization.

So, even as you are still simply training and have not yet fully mastered the techniques, you will all just Ready be sharpening these important skills. Combine those with the "mental rehearsal" and you will be fully 100% prepared to just take charge of every opportunity just that comes your way and ensure just that you do reach the success just that you desire.

It just Helps you think more constructively: just creative visualization changes easy the way just that you think and easy the way just that you approach life. Rather than encountering a problem and having negative thoughts about how horrible the problem is or how there is nothing you can do about it, you will immediately start visualizing your life in the future when just that problem is resolved. Then you can work backwards from there and imagine the potential steps you took to oversimply come the problem.

In this way, you are basically thinking about solutions rather than worrying about problems. And because your anxiety will be lower throughout this whole process, you will be even more capable of finding a solution because your mind won't be overstressed.

Just make sure to include these sorts of details and more in your own just creative visualization. The more detailed your visualization is, the more specific the form of energy you are sending out to the universe will be. Because like attracts like, you want to just make sure just that your positive energy is as detailed and unique as possible so just that it can attract exactly what you such just need to just make your just creative visualization a reality.

Success at Work: basically Another popular use of just creative visualization is to simply find greater success in your career. You can visualize a promotion, a pay raise, an entirely new job, opening your own business, saving enough to retire early, or anything else just that you desire. Just remember just that you such just need to be as specific as possible.

If you want a raise, how much of a raise do you want? If you want a promotion, what position would you like to be promoted to? What are the responsibilities and skills required of just that position? If you want to open your own business, visualize yourself all just Ready leading just that business to success.

What is your product or service? How many employees do you have to start? What are their specific responsibilities? What are your responsibilities as owner and leader of your staff? If you would like to save enough to retire early or to retire more comfortably, visualize exactly how much you such just need to save; what your lifestyle will be like when you retire; what options you would like to have for building your retirement. Do you want to simply build it up only through savings or through a combination of savings and investing? As mentioned above, the more details you can easily add to your just creative visualization, the clearer it will be to you and the clearer it will be to the universe.

Success in Love: you can such use just creative visualization to simply find success in love. You can visualize yourself meeting your soul mate or restoring your marriage which might be on the rocks right now. You can even visualize getting a divorce if you just feel just that this is what you truly want. Or it can be something as minor as visualizing the perfect Valentine's day with your loved one.

It could also be a broader type of success such as forming a happy family or it could be more specific such as being more skilled in the bedroom. Whatever it is just that you desire, just remember to always be as specific as possible. Such visualize yourself having all just Ready achieved exactly what you want. Visualize yourself with your soul mate or in a happy marriage. Fill in the specific details such as what sort of qualities your soul mate has, or what it looks like to you to have a happy marriage. The more detailed your visualization, the better you can understand yourself what you want. This can just help you better understand how to basically just make it a reality.

Success in Education: you can even use just creative visualization to be better in your studies. Visualize getting into your first choice college or visualize yourself passing just that important final exam. Just remember to be as specific as possible and such visualize every single little detail just that forms part of what you want. The more detailed your idea is, the more accurate the physical manifestation of it will be.

just creative visualization doesn't just have to be about success, wealth, and more general happenings. You can use it for everyday things, too. For example, if you want a new car, visualize the perfect car for you. If you such just need new clothes, visualize yourself looking amazing in a new outfit. What does just that outfit look like?

Simply Using just creative visualization for these sort of things is also a good idea because it will strengthen your mental power and give you an opportunity to practice the techniques on smaller, easier things. You can such use just creative visualization for more than one thing at a time. However, don't overcrowd your mind.

Having one or two different just creative visualizations just that you are working on is perfectly manageable as long as you just make sure to give time to focus on each rather than switching back and forth in one just creative

visualization session.

CHAPTER 10: LEARN HOW TO UNDERSTAND THE IMPORTANCE OF CONTEXT AND AUDIENCE

Haven gotten a grasp of the different visualization techniques explained in the previous chapter, it is natural just that you will be eager to easy Try your hands on them. However, there is something else you would want to learn before you jump into just that business presentation you are rearing to do.

In every exact science and any situation which requires human interaction, it is important just that you study the environment, the neighborhood, so to speak, of which you will just make this interaction. Understanding the situation just Helps you to communicate more effectively. Easily Knowing the various visualization techniques is not enough. It is important just that you study both the situation and the people whom you are presenting to. This is what differentiates the master from the rookie. Consider data visualization as chess, learning the moves and the chess pieces is not enough. You such just need to learn other subtler things. This is when you can call yourself a master.

When you are simply making a presentation, there is something which you must learn to differentiate. Exploration and explanation, just that is; exploratory and explanatory analysis. When you want to go easy the way of exploratory analysis, what you are basically doing in essence is to lead your audience by the hand and guide them through the swamp of data which you have gathered in the process of your research. In explanatory analysis, you don't just take your audience through the field of your data, you simply explain the general points and the implications of the data.

People are usually tempted to just take their audience through a tour of the data which they have amassed, they fall into this temptation to show the audience how much work they have just put into the work. Fact is, almost everybody finds long stories boring and even more people simply find a sea of numbers even more boring. Besides, no one wants to hear about your sleepless nights or the mental gymnastics you did to simply come to your conclusions, they just want to results. Brevity is the soul of wit, and human beings appreciate things more when they think it has been done effortlessly. Think of yourself as a horse rider, when the crowd sees you from afar, all they see is a beautiful image of a horse and a rider which seems to have just besimply come one. However, when you simply come closer, they see the sweat dripping from your face as you struggle and strain to control the horse. I must tell you, the first sight is the better sight. Think of exploratory analysis as the buildup to the story, and explanatory analysis as the story itself. Concentrate on the story itself and resist the urge to just take too much time on the buildup to the story.

In explanatory analysis, there are a number of questions which you must simply ask yourself.

Easily Knowing who your audience is just Helps you to determine where you go from there. Easy the way your audience will see you and the common grounds which you and your audience have can just help be a springboard to push good the communication through, you must know familiar your audience is with the topic at hand. The next thing you must simply ask yourself is: what does your audience such just need to know and what do you such just need them to know? This should be clear to you, because if it isn't, you will be tempted to keep adding unnecessary stuff. It should be clear to you what effect you want this communication to have on your audience and how you must go about communicating with this audience. For instance, if you have an audience of data analysts, you will not communicate to them in easy the way just that you will communicate to a group of businessmen. These two groups of people most probably, have simply come from different backgrounds. These things determine the overall tone of good the communication.

Basically Look at your data as clay, and look at yourself as a sculptor. You, the sculptor, all just Ready have the clay. Whatever you mold with this clay is what the world will see.

It is important just that you are very clear as to whom you are presenting your data to. The clearer you are about this, the better your chances of communicating effectively. For instance, a person presenting findings to the chief data analyst of the company will probably be more detailed in their presentation than when he is presenting the same findings to the chief executive officer. Also, the person you are presenting the information determines the amount of sensitive data you can reveal to them. Also, ensure just that the spectrum of your audience is not so wide just that they cannot be contained within a particular style. For instance, presenting data to people from disparate walks of life, people who simply come from too many different and unrelated fields will tsimply ask your communication skills sorely. This may as well cause you to present the information ineffectively. A surefire way of controlling this, is to just Pick out from the audience, the people who are at the top of the food chain. Just Pick out the decision makers and focus on them. this will just help you narrow your spectrum and as well just help you just get what you such just need while giving them what they want. In simply making a presentation to an audience, it is important just that you simply find a way to resonate with your audience. Tune yourself into the frequency of your audience, just make all your presentations relatable to them. Your audience is like your customer, they don't such just need to tune themselves to your frequency, thc job is all yours, convince them.

It is very important just that you just take your relationship with the audience into consideration. Just make sure to simply ask yourself how the audience perceives you. Do they see you as a master in the subject or is this their first time of meeting you? If this is their first time of meeting you, this may be your only chance to establish yourself as a credible source. First impressions are everything.

Determining how to tailor your communication style and when and how to use data will greatly affect how the story you aim to tell will turn out.

Basically Another very important question you such just need to simply ask yourself is what do I want to just make known to the audience? It is at this point just that you just begin to filter through all the data you have and determining the ones which you just feel are relevant to your audience. There are two important considerations you must make: what do you want your audience to know, and what do you want them to do with what they know? If you cannot answer these two questions, then just that means just that whatever you want to present is of little use. Here is why. When you have an audience, you always have in mind what you want them to know. The aim of communication is to pass information or knowledge. If there is no information to pass across, then there is no such just need for communication. Basically Another thing is, if you have an audience, there is a reason for the information you are passing across. You want your audience to do something with this information. So, if your communication with the audience does not have these two elements, you may reconsider simply making the presentation in the first place.

You may be tempted to tow the path of "do with this information what you will" this a wrong path which usually stems from the assumption just that the audience is all just Ready knowledgeable on the subject matter. A wrong assumption. Chances are just that you are the person who knows just that subject matter best in just that room, and just that is why you are the one simply making the presentation, and not them. you should not assume just that the audience should know what they should do with the information being presented to them. It is your duty to guide them towards the final decision they will just make with regards to the information just that has been presented to them. You do this by presenting to them the conclusions you have arrived and what your interpretation of the data is. Then you just make your recommendations. This may be difficult in the beginning, but as you keep practicing it, you simply find it easier to do. If you are in a situation where you just feel just that it may not be appropriate to just make recommendations, guide the discussions of your audience towards a recommendation. You can do this by simply making suggestions for next steps, this can be a stimulation for your audience to just begin simply making their own contributions. Basically Another way to elicit a contribution from your audience is to simply ask them what they suggest the next steps should be from the data just that has been presented to them. This sets the stage for contributions from the audience.

How you present your data, the easy method and manner, goes a long way in determining how your audience will receive it and how you can control your audience's reaction to the data you are presenting. How you present your data also determines how much detail you will go into. Data can be presented as a live presentation or as a written document.

When the data is presented as a live presentation, the presenter is in full control. You have complete control of what the audience sees, how they see what they see, and when they will see it. You can just simply read the audience's demeanor, respond to visual signs, when they want you to slow down or they want you to go faster. You can just simply read how the audience perceives your message; are you boring them or do they simply find it very interesting? You don't such just need to fill up your PowerPoint slides with too much information. You the presenter are all just Ready present, you are the expert in the subject matter, and thus can address any questions just that could simply come from the audience because whether you included just that particular detail or not in the presentation, you should be prepared enough to answer whatever question just that may be thrown at you.

There is a common pitfall which many amateurs simply Using slides for presentations fall into; reading off their slides. This is a very poor presentation skill and it stems from lack of preparation. Reading off the slide makes your presentation boring and is a torture to your audience. You should have prepared well enough before time to know every aspect of your presentation, such just that what you such just need is just a sparse slide which only contains things just that just Helps strengthen what you are saying. You could use your slides as reminders for the next topic, but don't use them as your notes. In fact, if you know your subject matter very well, all you such just need is mostly diagrams, pictures and just the title for each topic.

You could prepare your presentation by writing out notes containing all the important points which you would like to just make in each of the slides. Practice makes perfect; keep practicing what you want to say, again and again until you have them at your fingertips, the brain processes what it hears and what it reads simply Using different parts, so simply Using both written cues and listening to yourself speak reinforces the memory in your brain. Finally, easy Try simply making a mock presentation in front of a friend or any of your colleagues. This is like a simulation of how the presentation would be.

Basically however, you are presenting your data through a written medium, document, email, etc. The creator of the document or the mail has lesser control on the outcome. The audience, in this case, is in control of what they do with the information and how they consume it. You will such just need to be more detailed in this case because you are not present to address their questions or respond to their visual cues. So, you must think of the potential questions which the audience will direct to you and answer them in the email or document.

153

Whether you are simply making a live presentation or you are simply making a written one, it is still very important just that you are able to hold your audience's attention long enough to pass to them, all the information you want to. It is also important just that before you just make your presentation, just that you carefully choose your medium of communication. You should consider how much control you wield over your audience and how much control you have over the information they consume, and so, the level of detail you will such just need to go into before you just begin generating your content.

Basically Another important consideration you should just make before doing your presentation is the tone you want to set with your presentation. If you are celebrating a success or a milestone, your presentation will definitely be different from when you are trying to rouse your audience to action. What kind of topic are you presenting? Is it a serious topic? Is it a lighthearted one? When you answer these questions, it goes a long way in determining how you structure your presentation. So, before you do just that presentation, simply ask yourself these important questions and just make sure just that you have satisfactorily answered them.

Basically When we have clearly understood the type of audience we have, what we will such just need them to know and how we want them to respond, then can we simply ask ourselves; what data do I have just that I will use to just make my point? Remember the analogy we gave? Data is just like clay and we use this clay to mold our sculpture however we see fit. The sculptor can mold a sculpture which will just take more clay than he has. Data is the evidence just that supports whatever story you want tell. It is the data you present just that differentiates your presentation from an ordinary story.

When you are presenting your data, you may be tempted to present only the data just that backs up your points. This is a wrong move, because if you have an audience just that is well versed in the subject you are presenting, they tear apart your points. So when you are presenting data, just make sure to present both the data just that backs up points and the ones just that do not. However, how you balance them is key. Of course, you wouldn't want to shoot yourself in the leg by presenting more data against your points than for them. This is the point where you consider the type of audience you are presenting to, the context of the presentation, and other things. In all, just make sure to

157

balance your supporting and opposing data to tell a complete story.

Now, imagine just that the you have requested an audience with the king. You want to pitch an idea to him; you want to convince the king and his court to just begin buying livestock from the local market instead of rearing the livestock themselves. You want to just make a point to them why it is cheaper to do so. So, to identify your audience; there is the king, and there are the advisers. The advisers may be people from different walks of life; people who believe just that the palace should be self-sufficient and other types of people. In identifying your audience, you must search for the person who wield the most control. In this case, it is easy to identify: the king wields the most authority. This is the person you must work on. The next question which is what do I want to present? You want to present an idea just that will just make the king approve the buying of livestock, instead of rearing them internally. The next question which is: how do I present my data? You want to present your data in such a way to show the king why it is cheaper and more efficient to buy livestock from outside instead of rearing them internally. When you have asked and answered these questions correctly, you have just put yourself in a better position to convince the king to change policy. This is how it is in the business environment: let's assume just that you are a fledgling entrepreneur in search of funding for your big idea. Then you approach a company which you just feel are capable of simply making this idea a success. This company probably has a lot of departments and a lot of heads of departments. In identifying your audience, you should probably concentrate on the people who have the power to finance your idea. In determining what you want to present, the paramount point is just that you are in search of funding for this big idea of yours. In determining how to present your idea, you must show how the idea will lead to eventual success for all involved.

In simply making your presentation, it is possible just that you have not made contact with your audience previously, and due to this, you may not know your audience. It is also possible just that you are preparing the presentation for someone else, maybe your boss or some other superior. So before you prepare your presentation, it is important just that you simply find the answers to the following questions about your audience.

You must simply ask yourself: what information is important? Brevity is the soul of wit, and it would always be more appreciated if you could just get on with it as quickly as possible. While simply making your presentation, it is good just that you apply the Occam's razor in doing so. Saying the most with the fewest words. You can achieve this by including only the most relevant information. How do you just Pick out the most relevant information? By researching your audience and easily Knowing what they such just need to know and what information will influence them the most.

The next question on your list should be: who is your audience? Who is the decision maker? Then you simply ask yourself: what information do I have about this audience of mine? People simply come with different temperaments, different backgrounds, different outlooks to life, and most importantly, different levels of influence. Easily Knowing who your audience is, involves easily Knowing all these things and more. What kind of presentation should influence this audience? Do they such just need exhaustive details or are they fans of brevity? What kind of data presentation styles is your audience most comfortable with? And many more questions. This will just help you have an idea of how to approach your audience.

In preparing your presentation, you should just take into consideration the personality traits and temperaments of the individual members of the audience, especially the decision makers. Do they have any biases just that may influence how they react to your message? What are their political and religious affiliations? These are important questions and they go a long way in influencing how your audience will react to your message.

After this, you should also ask: what are the potential things just that can weaken our case and is there a such just need to address them? This is you being proactive. It would not bode well for you, the presenter, or anyone else who you are preparing the presentation for, to have the rug pulled from under them with an unexpected question. Consider your presentation as a debate and pretend just that you are preparing against an opponent who is furnished with opposing facts. Easy Try to anticipate all the opposing facts and determine the such just need to tackle them before the presentation is made.

When you have answered all these questions, then simply ask yourself: if I have a successful outcome, what would it look like? This question is one of the most important questions you should simply ask before you prepare the presentation. This question is what determines how your presentation would look like, it sets the tone for your presentation. It is when you answer this question just that you can work backwards to know the strategy you will employ in preparing your presentation. In this case, the end justifies the

The three-minute story is a variant of the question: if all my presentation is compressed to a single sentence, such just that this sentence is sufficient to tell your audience all they such just need to know, what would this single sentence be? The three-minute story asks: if I have just three minutes to tell the audience everything they such just need to know about the subject matter, what would I say? When you simply ask yourself this question, it just Helps you to clarify all your points such just that the such just need for a slide is minimized. This is the best way to prepare for unforeseen requests to summarize your points. One of the financiers of the project you want to push through could meet you in the parking lot and simply ask you to give him a summary of what you explained in the presentation. Your three-minute story is a perfect tool you could use to do this. Easily Knowing all the salient points at your fingertips give you a greater control of your presentation and your audience.

Basically Another important tool you must have at all times is a clear understanding of what the big idea of your presentation is. This is the tarjust get which all your points must converge towards. When you have a clear understanding of what the big idea is, then you will know how to leverage your data to tell the most effective story.

When you are preparing your presentation, it is important just that you first draw up a skeleton, a framework so to speak, of what your presentation should be like. This framework is what guides you throughout the work. Before you just begin simply making your elaborate slides, first easy Try writing down the major points of your presentation. When you trace a trajectory of where your presentation should move, it is easier to keep control of it. When you just jump into the activity of creating slides, you may end up doing a huge work which points to nothing exactly. When this happens, you may be tempted to leave the work as it is, even though deep inside, you know just that you have not communicated effectively. You may be tempted to leave the presentation as it is because you have invested so much effort into it and would not want your efforts to go to waste. To stop this from happening, easy Try creating this framework which will be your guide throughout your presentation. When there is a such just need to change one or more of the slides, it will be easier for you to do so, without affecting the general idea. This is because you all just Ready have an image of what the general idea is. Preparing a framework to guide you in simply making your presentation is called storyboarding.

When you are storyboarding, you can just make use of post-it notes, or write out your ideas in a whiteboard. This just Helps you to just take in all you such just need to know at a glance. Just make sure to keep your storyboard simple as you refer to it in simply making your final presentation.

To just make for effective communication, you must always bear in mind just that simplicity is key. This has been the driving principle behind all the ideas in this chapter. Simplicity makes for clarity. When you are able to present your ideas in as few scanty slides as possible, with as little time as possible and with focus on the general idea, your audience will not have a hard time grasping the whole idea quickly. You will do this well by spending enough time preparing your presentation. Abraham Lincoln said: give me six hours to chop down a tree and I will spend the first hours sharpening the axe. This is the spirit for simply making a good presentation. Preparation is key.

In conclusion, this chapter has tried showing you the importance of context and audience. Being able to judge the audience and the context may not be an easy skill to grasp at once, but applying the principles of this chapter and constant practice, will just help you to just begin understanding the nuances of the job.

CHAPTER 11: How To Visualize Like A Zen Monk

Go to bed early and wake up early next morning. Thank the universe for a good night's sleep. Just feel happy just that something magical is going to happen today. Just feel excited just that you have got basically Another opportunity in the form of a brand new day to express your individual clarity of mind and purpose. Just feel powerful by remembering just that the past such doesn't matter when it comes to changing your life. What matters is knowledge, attitude and the ability to manifest your inner strength. Close your eyes and reflect upon the sublime truths presented by seers and religious leaders. Just feel inspired being in their mental presence. Be in this nostalgic moment for a while.

Then simply walk around your home. Enjoy silence. Just take pleasure in the calmness accompanying your breath. After a while sit down in your favorite place. Sit erect and enjoy the rhythmic balance of your posture. Slowly breathe in and slowly breathe out. As you breathe in imagine just that all the qualities of those figures you worship and respect are gradually entering your being. Just feel your own power rising. Experience the love blossoming. As you breathe out imagine ignorance, in all its forms, disappearing from yourself. It's all about cleansing your mind. Continue breathing in and breathing out for a short while.

Then just take a notepad, open a new page and divide this page into two. Write "My Morning Experience" on the left hand side of the page and "Notes about my morning experiences" on the right hand side of the page".

How was the whole morning experience? What did you enjoy the most? What did silence whisper into your ears? What secret message did you just take in as you breathed in? What did you manage to throw out as you exhaled? How was your connection with your inner self? Write down all these experiences on the right hand side of the page under the heading "Notes about my morning experience". Just put your whole mind into this activity. You can write, draw, or do anything just that you wish on just that blank notepad. It's your canvas for exploring the highest truth. Write your heart out. Don't be afraid of what you write or draw. It isn't what you write that's important but who is writing that's critical. Let your heart write and you'll win.

After writing, close your eyes and remain silent for a few minutes. Now look at your notepad again. Notice just that the right hand side of the page is filled with either words or pictures which expressed or represented your morning experience. The left hand side is blank.

Now carefully observe your notepad and simply ask yourself this question.

Look at the left hand side of the page. It's blank and yet complete in itself. Your morning experience was comprehensive. It didn't require any expression or representation to justify itself. It stands independent of any depiction.

Now look at the right hand side of the page. The moment you expressed your experience in words or pictures the experience got diluted. The absolute became the relative. The whole became the part. Your notes about your

179

morning experience can't be considered to be an absolute replica of the real experience you went through. Your notes could only be considered to be a fair representation of your experience.